I0149491

THE THINGS WE LEAVE UNSAID

Haven King

ISBN: 979-8-218-25877-1

ACKNOWLEDGMENTS

To my family for their endless support & encouragement of even my wildest of dreams.

To L & P.P. for always reminding me of who I am, you all are the reason these words made it here.

To every other human, that I've loved and been loved by … you're all a part of this story in some way.

& Finally, to the girl I was before… this is for you. All the words that you never got to say or hear, lie here.

With love,
Hav

The Things We Leave Unsaid

These words are meant to heal and hold you.

These words are meant to diminish the isolation and acknowledge the feelings.

Some are texts never sent

While others are words never spoken…

Words to past lovers, past friends, and past selves.

Words needed to be said & others needed to be heard.

Words for the healed and for the hurting.

Words for everyone… for all of you.

I'll sit with you while you read them.

The Things We Leave Unsaid

It's…

the unreachable scratch… and insoluble itch
the answerless question and absent truth
the ellipsing thought and agonizing wonder

It's…

The Things We Leave Unsaid…

Sometimes I miss it.

The hurt.

The sleepless nights.
The chest heaves & shallow breaths.
The recurrent sobs & steady ache.

Because as much as it hurt.

I think I've forgotten what it's like to feel for someone that deeply.

Vulnerability

How strange it is…

It's the moments of its greatest strength
that often led us to its absence

I used to believe that in order to be made whole again,

all the wounds unhealed must close

But I've realized
it's in that space... the nursery of growth begins

What a funny thing it is

that the one thing I would say now is… thank you.
Because if it wasn't for you

I would never have known how capable I am on my own

After all this time

I am reminded of why I couldn't stay…
I see you, and I remember

I remember everything we could have been

The greatest loneliness
can only be found
in the most crowded of rooms

I always imagined the fall
with its subtly and softness

But it wasn't until the remnants
were scattered across the floor

I realized I had been falling all along

Sometimes "it will get better" is a hope
 other times a plea

 but still, we say it…because maybe, just maybe
deep down, we know if we say it enough,

 We'll believe it

So many times, relationships are described with such a definitive ending simply ending where it once began...

Moving from strangers back to strangers again.

But what a disheartening way to look at time spent with another human, seeping with the connotation of wasted effort & wasted time

Yes, you may not know the mundane details of one's everyday life as you once did, but does that truly warrant the estranged classification of a stranger?

Can someone you shared such moments of everlasting love and laughter with... ever really be a stranger?

 If that's so, I hope I meet a lifetime more of strangers just the same,

Don't you?

Trying to rewrite all the good
will only prolong the healing.
Seek to acknowledge it all...

There are both beautiful and tragic moments in every story.

I wish I would have savored it a little more

I wish I would have made the last hug a little tighter
the last laugh a little deeper,
the last smile a little wider,
and the last tear fall a little slower.

Whatever it is you are so greatly trekking toward will come
in time just as it is meant.

 But until then, savor the time in the now.

What's ahead will be, but what's now will never be again.

For the ones whose hearts and minds sit in opposition...

It's okay.
It's okay if you're angry that your heart still holds the love your mind knows you don't deserve. It's okay to still feel it all while simultaneously wanting more. It's okay for your mind to know not to settle & it's okay for your heart to wish you could.

It's okay if your heart is still holding on
to what your mind knows isn't meant for you.

Sometimes waking up
and choosing to keep going

is enough

People can be seasonal too

You may feel healed one day and broken the next

what a ruminating cycle this creates within us

Tethering the line
 between broken & whole

All we face is seasonal…

I hope those of you that read this with heaviness on your heart tonight know that one day the pain will lessen and the light will flood back in…with a greater appreciation & gratitude you've yet to know. I hope those of you feeling stuck… and trapped by the front you put on or the "smile" you wear know that one day, that charade you've been so perfectly performing will be replaced with the genuine joy you once knew. I hope you know that despite the impermanence of these times, your emotion and struggles still rightfully claim every piece of validity.

But most of all, I hope you chose nothing more than to keep going and believing in all that's to come

You'll find it.

You'll find the kind of love you can feel in your bones.
The kind you convinced yourself couldn't exist.
The kind you had given up on.
The kind of love you deserve.

But you must find yourself first.

To all the I love yous never uttered,

feelings unshared,
compliments left breathless,
and dreams unfulfilled...

I hope you find your way home.

I looked up to meet the eyes of the past.

But instead,
was met by a stranger

& I think that's how it was meant to be all along

You don't have to have it all figured out

not today, not tomorrow, not next month, or even next year

What's meant for you can't be rushed, what's meant for you will show itself...in time...

But only when you're ready

Maybe one day you'll find the answer

 or the "why" that makes sense of it all
or maybe you won't.

You get to heal regardless

People tell me to stop
To stop romanticizing what we had

But what if the romanticization

is the only thing I have left?

But what about all the people who stayed?

It's okay to miss someone who isn't good for you

That red shirt

You know the one.
From the night we met
with its tethered edges and faded outlines

That red shirt saw it
All of it

the laughter, the tears
the joy, the betrayal
the love
& the hate

There was a time when I felt it would be impossible to forget.

That color red burned into my memory and etched into the scars

But now, after all this was time

Was that shirt ever even red?

I hope you begin each day by breathing deep into your lungs
 grounding your feet in the earth

 & reminding yourself, despite everything,
you are deserving of a beautiful life

But there's still so much left for you…

Love still to be found &
Tears still to fall

Memories still to be made &
Butterflies still to be felt

Friendships still to be cultivated &
Hearts still to be opened

Hands still to be held &
Places still to be seen

Eyes still to be widened
& Minds still to be changed

Ideas still to be formed
& Proclamations still to be heard

The chapter may be ending

But you

You are just beginning

I hope you're okay
and this time
I mean it

If my soul could take another vessel

I hope it would be…in the daze of the first morning "hi"

   in the prolonged gazes across crowded rooms
   in the soft eye rolls and upward bend of the lips
   in the gratuitous coffees
   & the spontaneous bouquet
   in the simple hair strokes
   & gentle touches of the spin

If my soul could take another vessel

I hope it would be not in the grandiose moments of love
but in moments like these

Where love is alive.

Don't let others disturb your peace
just because they are not ready
to make peace of their own

This is for you.

For the person who has become so good at the charade. So good that you yourself even believe it at times.

Too good.

To the one who has perfected the plastered smile and the prerecorded laugh. The one who finds it easier to pretend than to burden others with the weight of your problems.

You deserve to find the genuine joy you once knew. You deserve to cry at life's unfairness and scream of your frustrations. You deserve to heal. But most of all you deserve to be given all it is you give to others.

"What does healing feel like?"
it happens...
as quickly as a blink
with the longevity of an eternity.

I think maybe my mind liked the confusion
because it meant there was still hope
It meant there was a world where we could wake up
not a single thing changed
but that world doesn't exist

It can't exist

I'm scared
I'm scared to feel nothing
even though it's what I wanted all along
What if I never find these feelings again?

What if I never find you?

My friends tell me they don't think I've experienced it

Love …real Love
But
I've known it all along

In the echoes of their laughs
& the warmth of their embrace
In the comfort of their voices
& the reassurance of their word
In the drying of my tears
& the holding of my hand

Everything I know about love

Love…real love
I found in them

There's a difference

between those who don't love you
And those who can't love you

Life is graciously beautiful, but life is also hard.

We crave connection fueled by relatability, something that seems unattainable when we're met with unachievable and unrealistic depictions of happiness for most.

Our timelines filled with stories of healing and resilience. Stories that are meant to inspire and reiterate this notion that if one just keeps moving forward, "it will get better." But what isolation that furthers when one is trapped in what feels like a revolving door of comparison and sadness. Thus a severance of connection begins; how is one standing in a room filled with people beaming with prideful perfection expected to share a story of such sorrow? The splendors of this fickle world are endless, but we seldom discuss the type of isolation that is bound to exist from the seamless narratives we are all fed.

All the while, we sit idly by encouraging people to ask for help and share their feelings...... a mere formality or a genuine inquisition?

Something no one talks about...

The juxtaposing emotions that arise from new beginnings. The contentment in one's decision to move on and the simultaneous mourning of what has always been known.

I was fighting for you...
Silly me for believing it was a fight I could ever win
After all…
I was fighting for someone who never even existed

I hope you find it
I hope you find it all,
everything that left your lips with me.
This is you
The you without me

To the person wondering why they aren't enough…

Wondering what more they could have done, what more they could have said, what more they could have to offer.

You're asking all the wrong questions, my dear. This was never about you. This was never about you at all.

Because at the end of the day, what you bring to the table doesn't change despite who's sitting across from you. Remember that.

The disheartening presence of finality seems to come at the time when we feel least ready.

But how special this is a difficult goodbye signifies a time filled with the most beautiful of moments.

The irreplicable laughter and unforgettable grins. The messiness of life and the exhilaration of youth. The uncountable memories and unforgettable nights. The tears. The joy. The sadness. The happiness. And all in between.

How lucky we are to have experienced something that makes the goodbye so hard

Maybe in another lifetime?

But I'm not sure I believe that either

Because there is no lifetime

In which I wouldn't have to convince you to love me

Growth and perfection are not synonymous, remember that

They tell you the person you think of when standing at the ocean is the one you love.

But I don't see someone else... I see her.

The same hair and the same eyes. But she's different. She is worldly yet soft. She is kind yet resilient. She is hungry yet content. She has loved and she has been loved. She has succeeded, and she has failed. She has laughed, and she has cried. She has celebrated, and she has mourned.

She has grown.

They tell you the person you think of when standing at the ocean is the one you love... and they are right.

But it's not the great love story, not yet at least... I'm falling in love with who I am becoming and who I want to be because standing at the ocean, I think of her.

The thing about falling for potential

is that it's only in the freefall
the ground in sight
that you realize the empty promises
and unrequited feelings are holding a sheet

not a parachute

There is a past version of you beaming with pride at how far you've come

Even though it may not seem like it,
the same will one day be true for this current moment.

Keep going

For the ones who turned the hurt into something beautiful...

you softened the harsh lines
shaped the muddled lessons
& gave meaning to the pain

But just because you made it into something beautiful...

Doesn't mean you deserved it in the first place

I loved you enough to let you go

But,

You didn't even love me enough to let me be

Life isn't about having everything figured out...

It's about falling for the wrong people and saying the wrong things. It's about taking missteps and choosing wrong paths. It's about putting effort into matters we know don't fulfill us and spending more time in underserving friendships and relationships than we know we should. It's about regret, apologies and mistakes.

This life was made for growth, discovery and learning, not perfection.

I don't believe in regret

I know all of this was meant to be a part of my story
Apart of me

I just wish the same was true of you

One day your side of the bed

Became nothing more than stale pillows and a wrinkled duvet

What heartbreak freedom brings

Making it through the valley doesn't erase the suffering...

there is just as much value in the hurt
as there is in the healing

You can grieve more in this lifetime

than just deaths

I know there will be another you, but I'm scared there may never be another me with you.

I miss her...

But I don't miss you.

From a distance, its appearance uniform and gray

But as the distance fades

the unique and distinctive features emerge

becoming evident

that what's depicted as the most universal of experiences

is drenched in loneliness and seeping of isolation

Grief is a fickle thing

I wonder if in 10 years

As the sound of little feet patter above & the dog whines through the screen door

I'll reach to click the pot on…

& suddenly be reminded of how you took your coffee

In case I see you one day in that same crowded bar
& all that can escape my lips are small pleasantries

Know that what I mean by "good to see you" is…

You made me feel seen
when I had yet to discover my own reflection
even despite the depth of the wounds
you left me to sew alone

That is something I will carry for the rest of this lifetime
and every one after

So, when I wish the best for you
and whisper quiet hopes of your happiness
Know that I mean it.

And know that, above all else,
I'll never regret meeting you.

Know that what I mean by "good to see you" is…

Thank You.

For the things you've left unsaid…

ABOUT THE AUTHOR

Haven King is an NYC based writer, poet, journalist and creative. Despite growing up in the small southern state of Arkansas, Haven has always chased bigger ideas, emotions, conversations and feelings. "The Things We Leave Unsaid" is Haven's debut poetry collection.